Mark, Diane, and

Roll y*our* rock!

Kcco,

R⬤LL THAT R⬤CK

A leadership book <u>NOT</u> for corporate America.

Clayton:
This book is dedicated to all
who dream of a better world
and are willing to spend their efforts
to make that dream a reality.
You inspire all of us to want a better world too.

Tony:
I dedicate this to all the Wise Williams
throughout my life and career...
those who rescued me when I was lost,
encouraged me when I was down,
and taught me when I was clueless.

Illustrations by Jeff Burkholder

ISBN: 978-1-7324130-5-4 (paperback)
ISBN: 978-1-7324130-6-1 (ebook)

Printed in the United States of America

1 2 3 4 5 6 7 8 9 10

For more information visit the authors online at:
RollThatRockBook.com
Facebook.com/RollThatRockBook

Why Does Your Group Even Need This Book?

A leadership book <u>NOT</u> for corporate America.

"Never doubt that a small group of thoughtful, committed citizens can change the world. Indeed, it's the only thing that ever has." ~ Margaret Mead

I could immediately see Tony's visceral reaction as corners of his mouth curled downward and his nose shot up in disgust when I uttered the words, "We should write a small group leadership book".

"The world doesn't need ANOTHER leadership book, Clayton", Tony replied with a forced smile, as if to hide his initial reaction.

"Yes, but this leadership book wouldn't be for corporate America", I shot back.

Tony's eyes narrowed a bit before he responded, "Then who would it be for?" Having anticipated Tony's reaction to my statement, I immediately rattled off my well-rehearsed pitch all in the same breath. "It would be a small group leadership book for all of the small volunteer and non-profit groups that are tirelessly working to make the world a little bit better place. You know, the local Lions clubs, the Boys/Girls Scout troops, the church youth groups, the high school booster clubs…".

Tony certainly looked more intrigued at this point, "Ok, I see where you're going with this, but what makes you think these sorts of groups even need a book on small group leadership?"

Ok, I admit, that question took me by surprise, so I had to wing my next response, "I see a lot of these small community groups doing a lot of great things. They are putting significant amounts of time, effort, talent, and in some cases money into community projects, often with minimal results. I think we could change that with a book that provides basic leadership skills and group management strategies. After all, we've both done this for years, and we both care to help others do it too."

Tony, now fully engaged by my enthusiasm for the project, smiled and said "Well, I'm really busy and you're swamped, so the timing couldn't be better. Let's get started next week!"

So this book is written for what we call "real world" groups and their leaders. By calling them that, we do not mean to imply that those who work and lead in a corporate setting are not doing real work, only that there is something artificial in many of those contexts that those serving smaller, mission-minded, service organizations neither experience nor fully understand. Their job is usually much harder, not well compensated, and supported with significantly fewer resources.

While we're sure there is literally an infinite number of significant differences between the world of corporate America and "real world groups", five major differences primarily stand out to me.

- Unlike corporate America, which has been traditionally organized in a military style, top-down pecking order hierarchy, team work in the real world groups is generally not highly structured; in fact, many real world groups are basically amorphous outside of the appointed leader of the group. This often presents unique challenges when it comes to assigning responsibilities or, worse yet, accountability.

• Real world group team work is generally ungoverned. Federal, state, and local regulations and laws for corporate America often serve as boundaries and guidelines shaping the path forward; however, this is often not true for real world groups making the path undefined and uncertain.

• Teams in real world groups are mostly derived organically, not hand-picked talent. Corporate America has literally created a cottage industry for hiring, evaluating, and training the exact type of talent required for any given project or goal, while most real world groups end up embracing the age-old kindergarten adage, "You get what you get and you don't get upset".

• Corporate America can muster vast resources to bear in a timely manner but most real world groups can barely find enough time to gather the necessary resources. Time is as much of a resource as money and in many cases more valuable. Avoidance of labor-intensive options and fear of time wasting missteps often dominate the decision making process of real world groups.

• Corporate America has clearly defined job titles, roles, and duties, whereas real world group teamwork requires members to wear multiple hats dividing focus, creating confusion, breeding frustration, and fueling exhaustion. Often the appointed leader in real world group has to be a primary "rock roller" and still find the time to get down to the business of being an actual leader as well.

With all of the clear advantages corporate America has over these loosely structured, ungoverned, underfunded, mix and match group of misfits all playing so many roles they will probably develop an identity crisis, it is no wonder why so many real world groups struggle to "roll their rock" across the finish line, but yet…. in many cases, they still do.

This book is for all the volunteer and non-profit groups who dismiss all of the advantages of corporate America and find the heart and grit to roll their rock, but a little faster and with less fighting along the way.

Thank you for what you do to make the world a little better place for us all.

R⬤LL THAT R⬤CK

A leadership book NOT for corporate America.

DR. CLAYTON J. STITZEL
DR. TONY BLAIR
with PAUL DE ROSE

WILLIAM'S WISDOM

William is wise. William has gained his wisdom the hard way—by failing, and then succeeding, at leading rock-rolling teams. You'll meet him later in this book, when he will have some wisdom to share with our main character.

But he also has some wisdom to share with you! Throughout the story, these boxes of "William's Wisdom" will point you to what leadership practitioners and scholars have learned over the years about how to lead, and how to lead teams in particular. William will also recommend further reading for you, if you want to explore some of his wisdom more fully.

Behind the   Lee   Gloria   Scott   Matt
Scenes   the   the Glory-   the   the
Bob   Leader   Hound   Squatter   Martyr

The large conference room was standing room only. And everyone knew why they were there. The group looked at each other - some whispering, some in still silence. The urgency in the room was palpable.

It was that project. That overwhelming project, the one that always loomed in the background. Always the elephant in the room. It was like a huge 'ROCK' in everyone's way, but no one knew what to do about it. And it was far too large for any one person to move. This would need to be a team effort. A giant effort to Roll this Rock out of the way once and for all.

Whatever anyone thought about the project itself, one thing was clear: This Rock wouldn't go away on it's own. Someone was going to have lead a team to Roll this Rock in a new direction and to its final destination. Permanently.

WILLIAM'S WISDOM

WHAT'S YOUR ROCK?

All of us have a rock to move. It may be a project or task at work, or a personal goal (such as to lose weight or finish school). The most challenging rocks, however, are those that we roll with others, especially when we're the ones called to lead. You might call rolling those rocks your objective, your goal, your vision, or your mission; leadership books speak of all those things. At this point, however, it doesn't matter so much what we call them... the reality of the rock in front of us is what matters most. How can we work together to get it where it needs to go?

If you're a leader—voluntarily or not—and you've tried in the past to get others to move a rock without the success you hoped for, or if you have a rock staring at you and your team right now, or if you are pretty sure you'll have to deal with one in the future, read on! This story is for you!

The door opened, and in walked someone who looked like he was in charge. He had an entourage at his side. He walked to the empty spot at the head of a large oak table and slowly opened a file folder.

"The writing is on the wall. And let's be honest, we all saw this coming. The Rock of a project we've all feared is here and is not going to move on its own - as much as we would like it to. This Rock needs to be rolled in a new direction. Permanently."

"Somebody needs to step up and handle this."

The Man in Charge continued, "We need someone capable and competent. Someone with experience to head this project up. And I can think of only one name."

Everyone looked around. A bright-eyed man at the other end of the table quickly shot up his hand. "Me. I'm that man. I'm capable and experienced, but most of all, I have a passion for rolling. I will roll it!" he exclaimed.

The others turned simultaneously in surprise to glare at the man, whose name was Leland.

As you may have guessed, Leland was an extremely confident man. "Well, as most of you should know, I have a great track record of rock rolling. I've moved some pretty influential rocks in my day. Not to be a Rock dropper, but I've worked with the best names in the business."

WILLIAM'S WISDOM

WHO'S THE LEADER?

Lee wants to lead. Is eager to do it, actually. Not all of us are. Some of us find ourselves in leadership roles without asking for them. And sometimes, like Lee, we willingly take on projects without knowing fully what we're getting ourselves into. Have you had this experience? Have you ever been a leader by accident, default, or deception?

If so, how do you step up to the plate when you find yourself in charge and realize you don't know what to do? The good news is that leadership can be learned, and there's lot of help to learn it, including this book and the others we recommend here.

For further discussion, see *The Accidental Leader: What to do When You're Suddenly in Charge*, by Harvey Robbins and Michael Finley.

"To be honest, I was hoping that you would volunteer!" said The Man in Charge. "In fact, I was counting on it. Congratulations, Lee. You're the leader."

After the meeting, Lee was going on and on about his resumé, telling rock-rolling stories to anyone who would listen. He was cut short when The Man approached. "It's time to go out to the field and see your new Rock, Lee."

The Man in Charge led Lee out to a large field where many rocks of varying shapes and sizes sat. Some Rocks were being rolled by a team. Some just by one lonely person. Some rocks seemed stranded near the edges of the field, as if they had once been rolled partway but, for whatever reason, had stopped. Other rocks, bigger ones to be sure, had clusters of people around them, pushing, grunting, shouting, and even arguing.

WILLIAM'S WISDOM

HOW BIG IS YOUR ROCK?

Sometimes we find ourselves in over our heads because we have underestimated the scope of the work. There are several reasons for this. One is "mission creep," the phenomenon of seeing the project expand after it is initially engaged until it no longer has a core focus, and the people involved with it are not entirely sure why they are doing what they are doing. Mission motivates. Creep cripples. Keep it focused, and always remember to tell them (and yourself!) WHY they are doing what they are doing.

Another reason is that we let our hopes and aspirations overrule our eyes. Very few of us are entirely objective or rational; we tend to see what we want, and not what is. The best way to be sure that you're dealing with reality (before you say "yes" to something!) is to invite someone else – someone with no agenda of their own – to give you their assessment of the size and value of the project.

(continued on the next page...)

(HOW BIG IS YOUR ROCK continued...)

In fact, invite more than one "someone" to do that for you, as each of us look at things, especially our organizations, through certain frames or lenses. These frames give us clarity about what we're seeing directly ahead of us but can also serve as blinders, preventing us from seeing other aspects of the picture. The more frames through which you look, the more perspectives you can engage, the more information you'll have to make a clear decision.

For further discussion, see *Reframing Organizations: Artistry, Choice, and Leadership*, by Lee Bolman and Terrence Deal.

Before long, Lee the Leader (a self-appointed title that seemed to have a nice ring to it) spotted the Rock. His Rock. His innate confidence grew even more as he viewed it from a distance. *It's not as big as they let on! I'm going to get this done in no time,* thought Lee. But as he got closer and closer, the Rock got larger and larger until it loomed above him as a massive, unyielding boulder.

Standing in the shadow of the rock, Lee had one penetrating thought: *I will need help!*

Hmmm . . . who can help me most? thought Lee. The first face to come to mind was that of Behind the Scenes Bob. Lee had already worked on several projects with Bob. Not only was he a longtime friend, but he actually knew quite a bit about Rock Rolling. He was a multi-tasker. Bob had real credibility, and Lee held credibility in high regard. "Bob is the perfect person for me to lead!" he exulted.

WILLIAM'S WISD⬤M

GETTING REAL ABOUT MOTIVES

Bob is a take-charge kind of guy. You know the type. Maybe you ARE the type! If you're going to lead a team, Bob's the kind of person you'd want on that team. He gets things done. He doesn't cause drama. But if you're in it for your ego, Bob will sniff that out. He will lose trust in you, and probably outshine you. So this is a good time to ask yourself some hard questions about your own motives for leadership:

- WHY are you pushing this rock?

- Why are YOU pushing this rock?

- Why are you PUSHING this rock?

- Why are you pushing THIS rock?

(continued on the next page...)

(GETTING REAL ABOUT MOTIVES continued...)

Until you have a clear answer to each question, you will be ineffective as a leader. Note that, for most of us, our initial answers will contain a bit of self-deception, as none of us are entirely awake to our true motives. Invite others into this discussion, as they may help you see your blind spots and your ulterior motives.

For further discussion about the motives of leaders, see *Leadership and Self-Deception* by The Arbinger Institute.

So Lee marched resolutely back through the field, back through all the rocks of varying sizes, looking for Bob. After a short while, he came upon his old friend. Bob was surrounded by a handful of people who were apparently supposed to be pushing not one, but three, good-sized rocks! Bob was intently giving direction to a few of them, but others were shouting at him energetically. Some team members looked happy to be there, but most did not. And, as Lee looked closely, Bob did not appear to be very happy either.

Lee approached, and Bob spun to face him. "Lee! What a surprise! How goes it? Do you need help rolling a rock, by any chance? I can certainly squeeze another Rock into my schedule." He leaned in and whispered, "To be honest, I'm a little frustrated with these particular rocks – and these particular rock rollers."

Lee was ecstatic. He explained to Bob about his new project and how Bob could help.

WILLIAM'S WISD☁M

WHAT IS A GREAT LEADER?

This question, strangely enough, has perplexed leadership scholars for decades. For most of human history, it was sort of assumed that leaders were born, not made, and therefore it wasn't worth a whole lot of effort to try to train leaders; one either had leadership traits or one didn't. Today that attitude it called the "great man theory of leadership" or "trait theory." It's not very well respected by scholars but is still fairly common among ordinary people.

After World War II, which was a great laboratory to observe the benefits of good leadership (and the costs of poor leadership), people began researching leadership effectiveness in earnest, and concluded that leadership was not about inborn traits after all, but about certain skills and behaviors, which could be taught. Today you can see this focus in many of the leadership training workshops and seminars that are offered in the workplace and elsewhere; they're offering to teach you practical skills that will make you a more effective leader. And they may.

(continued on the next page...)

(... GREAT LEADER continued...)

By the 1970s, however, the focus had shifted again. Instead of looking at the leader in isolation, this approach sought to understand what kind of relationships between leaders and followers work best to accomplish goals. This seems to be the assumption of Leland the Leader in this story; how can he best motivate or work with Bob to get and keep the Rock rolling to its destination?

Other theories developed at about the same time focused neither on the leader or the follower but on the context in which they operated. They argued that leadership effectiveness is about getting the right person in the right position, or even getting the leader to adjust his or her style, depending on the context. It was all about context. And they had a point too.

Or maybe leadership effectiveness is about being authentic. Instead of presenting oneself as a heroic figure, perhaps we should all admit our weaknesses, failures, and fears, so that others will respect us as individuals and follow us anyway. The "authentic leadership" model is very popular today.

(continued on the next page...)

(... GREAT LEADER continued...**)**

Perhaps there is no one correct answer; perhaps effectiveness is a combination of a variety of factors—some having to do with the leader as a person, some arising from the skills a leader has learned along the way, some the result of the interactions between leaders and followers, and some reflecting the context in which all are operating. If so, it's a far more complicated equation than we're often told by popular books on leadership, and a bit messier than Lee the Leader seems to think at this point in the story.

Here's the encouragement: If you're not sure how to be an effective leader, you're not alone. Even the scholars don't know for certain. The point of this book, however, is that even if you don't have it all figured out, your followers will tell you through their own behaviors much of what you need to know to lead them well. Pay attention to them. But it might not hurt to familiarize yourself a bit more with some of the key leadership models. Leadership is an art, but art can be perfected.

For further discussion on leadership models and theories, see *Leadership: Theories and Models*, by Peter Northouse.

"I'm in!" said Bob. "Now I don't know if you remember, but I like to jump in to the deep end. Yep, I'll jump right in alongside you, Lee, and then go from there. I like challenges but I like to juggle many different projects at once. My execution is spot on, but my bedside manner could use some work. Of course, if things aren't moving like I think they should, or as fast as I think possible, I will take control from you. But it's just to make sure things get done right, of course! I'm a man of action! The problem is, most leaders don't know what to do with someone like me."

But all Lee heard was: "I'm in!"

So an excited Bob went out with a delighted Lee to the field of rocks. When they arrived at The Rock, Bob did jump right in, just as he had said. He wasn't intimidated at all by its size. And just like that, the Rock started to roll, and at quite a clip too! Lee and Bob had enjoyed quite a few achievements in their careers, and their experience was certainly showing now. It was just like old times.

At this moment Lee felt very proud of himself for being such a great leader.

As Lee the Leader and Behind the Scenes Bob continued to roll, strategize, and smile, a sharp-dressed woman suddenly appeared alongside them. She was smiling widely and held in her hands the largest smartphone they had ever seen. She walked briskly alongside the rolling Rock. "Looks like things are going well! I can that see you are making great progress on your project. To me, that means everything! I'm Gloria the Glory Hound. I show up when things are going well and I push myself into evident success stories. I love to get attention and admiration when things are good, and then disappear and place blame when things go bad."

WILLIAM'S WISDOM

DO YOU HEAR WHAT I HEAR?

Just like Bob and Gloria, team members "tell" leaders what kind of people they are, and how they will act, from the very beginning. This "telling" is not so much through their words as through their actions. Actions reveal much about how a person believes, values, and intends.

If we were but to "listen" better to what people tell us through their behaviors, we could all be better leaders. However, most leaders tend to "hear" what they want to hear, not what is necessarily true, and so deceive themselves.

(Continued on the next page...)

(DO YOU HEAR ... continued...)

What have the people on your team told you about themselves that you haven't paid attention to yet? What are they communicating through their resistance, their enthusiasm, their inability to work together, or their incredible ability to get done what you thought they couldn't? And what would they say if you asked some questions along those lines?

For further discussion about listening, see *Maestro: A Surprising Story about Leading by Listening*, by Roger Nierenberg.

But all Lee heard was: "Looks like things are going well!"

"Why don't I send a quick email to tell everyone how well we're doing?" Gloria said. "Done." In two seconds, Gloria had a glowing memo of self-praise sent to Everyone That Mattered - and even a few who didn't. It was signed "Gloria - Rock Rolling Liaison."

"Well, welcome to the team, I guess," said Lee.

"Why, thank you." she blushed. "This will be a great project to stay with until it falls apart and then I'll quickly move on to another.

WILLIAM'S WISD⬤M

WHAT IS YOUR DEFINITION OF SUCCESS?

What is "good enough"? Many of the conflicts of organizational life arise from competing but subjective understandings of what is good. One person is satisfied with a certain level of quality, and another is not. One decision-maker believes a particular design looks more professional, and another does not. One manager tolerates a certain level of imperfection, and another does not.

On one level this is a question of metrics. In many circumstances, "good" can be measured in terms of parts per million, sales per quarter, average response rate, percentage of loss, units manufactured per hour, etc. The International Organization for Standardization (IOS) has helped to quantify countless practices, particularly in the business sector, that can allow or even encourage organization to certain standards of quality. This can help immensely when such objective measurements are possible.

(Continued on the next page...)

(DEFINITION... continued...)

On another level, however, the challenge is less that of measuring quality and more a matter of our will to pursue it. One of the favorite dictums of the authors of this leadership fable is "the greatest hindrance to the best is the good." Most of the time we do not have to choose between "bad" and "good," and when we do, we know well enough to reject the bad and prefer the good. The harder choice is between "good enough" and "even better than this," because most will settle for what is merely good enough at the moment, especially when going for the best requires a disproportional amount of extra energy. But best is best.

Sometimes "good enough" truly is "good enough." But if it becomes normal, if it's our usual standard of success, we will never become great.

For more discussion, see *Good to Great: Why Some Companies Make the Leap...and Some Don't*, by Jim Collins.

Bob sharply looked at her, then back at Lee.

Gloria grinned, "Isn't life about presentation after all?"

Bob turned toward Lee wearing a curious smirk, but Lee hadn't heard a thing she said.

So Lee the Leader, Behind the Scenes Bob, and Gloria the Glory Hound worked together to roll the Rock. Actually, it was more like Bob and Lee rolling the Rock, and Gloria off to the side, tweeting furiously about rolling the Rock.

The Rock was rolling, but slowly. Lee glanced at the time and wished that they could go faster. In fact, if they were to reach their goal, they really *should* be going faster. This bothered him, but after all, the Rock was rolling forward little by little. And that was good enough for now.

They continued like this for some time. One day, when the three of them weren't making any real progress, and it seemed that the Rock would never get to the final destination in time, Lee took a much needed break to stretch his legs and think things over. Leaving the path, he traipsed across fields and streams while his mind raced.

Lee thought and thought about how they could make the Rock roll faster. He walked and thought. Thought and walked. Lost in his musings, Lee suddenly realized that he was standing in front of a beautiful home in the middle of the woods. Lee squinted and glimpsed an old man with a long white beard rocking contentedly in a chair on the porch.

This was no doubt the home of William the Wise!

William used to roll Rocks once upon a time and he became very, very good at it too. In fact, he had been celebrated as the best Rock Roller for fields and fields, for as long as anyone could remember. Anyone who knew Rocks knew that William was the go-to guy, the voice of wisdom. In fact, that was how he got his name. Or so the story went.

WILLIAM'S WISDOM

WISE GUY

Some people are wise and everyone just knows it. How does that happen? What makes a leader wise? It's more than mere experience, isn't it? It's been said that some people have 20 years' experience and others have one year of experience 20 times over!

It must be what we do with our experience that makes the difference – how we let it teach us, how we ourselves are changed in the process of leading change. Wisdom comes only to those who are brave enough to do the hard and humble work of personal, inner transformation. Increasing numbers of leadership experts are suggesting that spirituality can be a significant help with this... becoming a whole person, and living out that wholeness in your life both inside and outside of the workplace. If you want to change an organization, start by changing yourself.

For further discussion about being changed before we can change others, see *Deep Change: Discovering the Leader Within* by Robert E. Quinn.

"Hello, stranger!" called William. "I saw you rolling a Rock down yonder. I used to roll Rocks a long time ago."

Lee was excited to meet this fascinating old man. As he approached, he noticed a giant Rock nestled by the home. What a Rock it was too! It looked stately. Magnificent. Beautiful. Like it belonged there.

William invited Lee onto his porch. "Yes, come closer. I know things about Rocks, Lee."

Lee did walk closer and waited expectantly for the old man to continue, but Wise William took his time. Finally, he spoke.

"I know that you are up to this task. You've got what it takes to be a good leader."

Lee looked confused. He thought to himself, *Well, I know that too. I didn't think that was in doubt.*

William continued, "You have a good reputation for getting things done. But rock rolling is a very interesting business. It requires teamwork. No one can roll a rock alone. And the bigger the rock, the more necessary others are. Many leaders do not understand how to recruit good team members or how to get the most from the ones they have."

"Good leaders will lead each person differently. Some will jump right in while others will need some extra motivation. Some will know what to do while others need to be guided carefully. But I'm sure you know all of this already."

But Lee wasn't listening. All he heard was: "You have a good reputation for getting things done." And that made him smile.

"How can I make my Rock roll faster?" Lee jumped in. "And how far it is to my destination? I'm in a hurry to get this project done. I want to get back to the field and take on an even bigger, more important Rock next!"

William the Wise looked at him curiously. "At this point, you should not be concerned at all about your next Rock. This project requires your full attention."

"Uh, okay, then how can I get it moving faster? Is there a shortcut around here somewhere?"

"You are not listening," said William. "There is only one thing for you to be concerned about right now: Building an effective team. This is your priority as a leader."

"Well, I know that. Obviously," snarked Lee.

William the Wise stood up. "Oh, I'm glad to hear that. Then you should also know that each person who joins your team will tell you who they are – right from the beginning from their own mouth, and then again later with their actions. They will tell you where or even if they fit on your Rock-rolling project."

"Yes, it is your job to coordinate their efforts, but above all you need to let your best people be who they already are. That will be the secret to your success. Therein lies the Great Truth."

WILLIAM'S WISDOM

THE GREAT TRUTH?

There is nothing particularly mysterious about "The Great Truth," nor is it unique to William the Wise (or the authors of this volume). But it is so routinely overlooked that we call particular attention to it here. So much is made in the popular literature and training on leadership about "getting the right people on the bus and in the right seats," and "getting the most out of your people," and "aligning people and resources."

All of this is good and necessary, but leaders often respond with perplexity, because while they honestly want to do these things, they don't necessarily know how. That is why The Great Truth is such good news! You, the leader, don't have to figure all of this out by yourself. Your people will tell you themselves how, where, and when they will best serve!

(continued on the next page...)

(THE GREAT TRUTH continued...)

Of course, it's easier to say that than to do it. Many people are not terribly self-aware and don't know, consciously, the answers to these questions. But they will tell you by deeds, if not by words, their level of commitment, their level of compliance, and their level of collaboration with others. With this information alone, you can decide if they truly do have a role on your team, and if so, under what circumstances and in what capacity.

This is why we recommend that all hiring decisions (new hires for the organization and even decisions about whom to invite to join a project or work team) be accompanied by what's called a "behavioral interview." The standard resume is mostly about self-marketing and is therefore helpful only in the initial stages of a hiring process. And an interview about what a person "likes" to do or "will do" is rather useless, as past behavior is the best indicator of future performance. But this is what hiring processes often look like, particularly in the nonprofit sector.

(continued on the next page...)

(THE GREAT TRUTH continued...)

A behavioral interview, on the other hand, asks questions like this: "Tell me about a time when you faced unexpected major hurdles in accomplishing a goal. What were those hurdles and how did you deal with them?" If you are the interviewer, listen closely to the story chosen, the analysis offered by the interviewee (e.g. Did s/he take responsibility for his/her own actions or continually shift blame to others? Do you see evidence of strategic thinking? Of creative problem-solving?), and the learning that resulted.

Whether they intend to or not, people really do tell us who they are, what they value, how they work, and what they are passionate about...if we're willing to listen and observe.

For more information on using behavioral interviews, see *Hiring Talent: Decoding Levels of Work in the Behavioral Interview* by Tom Foster.

Lee looked puzzled. He thought to himself, *Well, the old man sure is full of information!* But the more he pondered, the more skeptical he became. After all, William was old, and he had been out of the game for quite some time. Did he even know what it was like out there in the field anymore?

However, William had a gleam of Something Good in his eyes when he spoke. Lee did like that, even though he wasn't quite sure what it meant.

"I don't know... I've gotten this far doing things my way," said Lee.

Wise William just smiled ruefully. "Then have it your way. Just be warned: You will have to deal with this sooner or later."

Lee spouted, "If you are so wise, then why is there still a large Rock in your yard? If you didn't reach your own goal, maybe you should stop preaching to others!"

WILLIAM'S WISDOM

WHERE IS YOUR HOUSE?

William's house represents the repository of wisdom to which his journey has led him. It's his home base, the source of what he now has to offer the world.

We all have a "house," our own home base. When we're younger, it's a very temporary dwelling. We haven't gained enough wisdom yet to offer much to others; we're still searching for it ourselves. Some continue in this pattern even in their old age, because they have accumulated much experience but still not much wisdom. If I build my house by a Rock that is not yet where it ought to be, the house itself will feel incomplete and out of place.

(continued on the next page....)

(WHERE IS YOUR HOUSE continued...)

But if I have had the experience of seeing at least one significant dream come true and knowing that I have provided some leadership to that endeavor—that I have struggled, failed, grown, been wounded and become wise in the process of achieving something worth doing—then I have a place to stand, a place to reside, a source of wisdom that I can now offer to others. This is my "house." And it is, to some degree, indestructible, for its foundation is Life itself.

This is what William has done. He is "retired" from the actual rolling of rocks but he is not "done." He has earned the right to say things, and to be listened to when he does. And he has built his house beside his rock, for that is how he came to be there in the first place.

Whose house are you visiting for wisdom? And where are you building your own house?

There are many books that attempt to capture the wisdom of those who came before us. One helpful anthology is *The Ten Golden Rules of Leadership: Classical Wisdom for Modern Leaders*, by M. A. Soupios and Panos Mourdoukoutas. There are also many wise people, like William.

The gleam in William's eye turned a bit dark. "That Rock is exactly where it's supposed to be. We rolled it to its own Finish Line. I built my house beside the Rock, not the other way around."

Taken aback, Lee stared hard at William, trying to figure this old wizard out. He certainly gave Lee much to think about. Much to think about indeed. With a wave of his hand toward William, Lee the Leader turned his back and hurried back to his Rock.

As Lee returned from a break that had lasted much longer than anticipated, he saw from a distance that his Rock was moving in his absence, albeit slowly. How was that possible? As he drew closer he saw that two other people were rolling the Rock beside Behind the Scenes Bob. Gloria the Glory Hound watched ecstatically.

When Lee arrived, Gloria ran excitedly to him, smartphone grasped in her flailing arms. "Look who came to help me!"

WILLIAM'S WISD☉M

WHICH WAY ARE WE GOING?

Missy Misguider is probably a familiar character for those of us who have worked in organizations for any length of time. She is enthusiastic, but somewhat clueless about how to use her energy in the most useful way. In a staff position, Missy can be directed if she has a wise manager. But sometimes, for reasons that baffle others, the Missy Misguiders of our organizations end up in management positions themselves, or even as CEOs.

The result is that a department, or the entire organization, flits in one direction, then reverses itself, then moves in an entirely new direction as new ideas or opportunities distract the leader from the stated objective. Other team members tire of "reading the tea leaves," that is, attempting to guess where they'll be headed next. Energies end up being dissipated, good will is squandered, and morale suffers under such an approach.

(continued on the next page...)

(WHICH WAY ARE WE GOING? continued...)

It is a leader's responsibility to point the way forward for the organization, walk in that direction, and to continue walking forward until or unless there is a rare but necessary reason to change directions. Inflexibility is not a virtue, but neither is indirection. Missy (and others) need to know in what direction they are to roll their rocks, and why. When they do, they are tremendous assets to any endeavor.

For more discussion, see *Get Everyone in Your Boat Rowing in the Same Direction: 5 Leadership Principles to Follow So Others Will Follow You,* by Bob Boylan.

Bob stopped pushing, caught his breath, and said to the two newcomers, "Well, I guess it's time to introduce yourselves more fully, now that the Leader is here."

"Oh, we thought you were the leader…" the woman exclaimed.

"Well, never mind that," Bob interrupted. "This is Lee. He's our Leader."

The vibrant woman shook Lee's hand vigorously. "Hi, I'm very excited to join your team! I'm Missy Misguider and I love to roll rocks! The truth is, most of the time I don't really know what I'm doing. Nor do I have a strategy. I just love being here, in the thick of things, even if it causes everyone around me more work. In fact, I will probably slow you down in the long run. My poor listening skills and poor sense of direction will frustrate everyone on the team."

But all Lee heard was, "I am very excited to join your team!"

"And who are you?" Lee inquired in the direction of the other newcomer.

"They call me Scott the Squatter. I know I could be a great rock roller, but I'm usually not terribly concerned about rolling rocks. To put it plainly, I'm in this for me. When my self-interest is accomplished, then I'll be done with your project. But as long as your Rock takes me where I want to go, I'm in. I just happened to be going your way. "

WILLIAM'S WISD😊M

IS MISSION THE REAL MOTIVATOR?

Leaders like to tell themselves that their people are "in it for the mission," whether that be the statement concocted by a committee that, if we were to be honest, looks very much like the mission statement of nearly every other organization in town, or the "real" mission that actually determines how decisions are made and funds are spent.

Those leaders are partially correct. Some are in it for the mission—they find meaning in what the organization does and have a deep commitment to making it better. But most aren't. Most of the thousands of people who work for financial services companies, for instance, did not grow up dreaming about sitting in a cubicle helping other people get more wealth. They work for such companies because the pay is good, or the hours are right, or the location is convenient, or some other perfectly worthy and rational reason.

(continued on the next page...)

(IS MISSION... continued...)

In fact, no one's motives are entirely unmixed, and even those who believe passionately in what the organization is doing will sometimes quit or falter, because they also have self-interest involved. For their own reasons, some who are there out of self-interest are willing to work very, very hard and offer much to the organization. Others, like Scott the Squatter, prefer to do as little as possible, and only in the areas in which their own self-interest explicitly coincides with the interests of the organization.

There are really only two ways to motivate them to greater involvement—either inspire them with a better reason by selling them on the true mission of the organization (i.e. help them find an intrinsic motivation), or appeal to their self-interest in every way possible (give them greater extrinsic motivation).

In the 1960s researcher Douglas McGregor labeled these two approaches "Theory X" and "Theory Y." The concept is overly dualistic but is a good starting point for understanding why you and the people you work with have chosen to work there, to do "that", and to pursue "this" career.

Since then, researchers have discovered that our motivations are much more complex, and often tied to cultural or family factors of which we might be mostly unconscious. In his book *Outliers: The Story of Success*, Malcolm Gladwell asks (and answers), "What makes high-achievers different?"

As usual, Lee didn't hear this any of this. He was thinking to himself, *With these two new recruits, I can get the Rock rolling faster! This is wonderful! Now, I should give them some orientation to our project…*

But before Lee could even open his mouth, Bob jumped in. "Well, enough chit chat! Let's get back to rolling this Rock! Keep going, just like I taught you."

Well of all the little… thought Lee. But the Rock started moving. Faster than ever before. Lee shrugged, put his own shoulder to the task, and thought happily of how he would be praised by The Man in Charge at the conclusion of this project.

But progress wasn't smooth. For some reason, the Rock kept careening off the path. But they would push it back on the trail and continue.

It seemed now to Lee that the Rock grew heavier. He had to work a lot harder to keep it rolling at the same speed, and he wondered why. But it was moving, and he was content with that for the moment.

And so it went for a while. But, then, suddenly, the Rock hit something. It stopped dead. They pushed and grunted and even swore, but it wouldn't budge. Scott yelled down from the top of the Rock, "It's a man!" Lee was so startled by this that he forgot to wonder why Scott was squatting on top of the Rock, or how long he had been there.

Scott was right. Lying in the middle of the road, right in front of the Rock, was a man.

WILLIAM'S WISD🪨M

ORGANIZATIONS CAUSE PAIN

Many of us have been hurt by organizations and especially by their leaders. This should not surprise us. Organizations are comprised of people, and people sometimes do horrible things to each other. Leaders are people with power, and power in the wrong hands has been known to be dangerous. Let us remember here Lord Acton's quip that "power corrupts, and absolute power corrupts absolutely."

The question, then, is not IF organizations will hurt their own people, but how such harm can be mitigated and even redeemed. Is there a way to minimize harm and maximize joy?

(continued on the next page...)

(ORGANIZATIONS... continued...)

Matt the Martyr represents all those who have been harmed so badly that they passively or even actively resist the work of the organization that hurt them...or any organization in which they become involved in the future. Sometimes their motives are at least partially altruistic—they want to spare others the pain they themselves have experienced. Sometimes, however, they are mostly concerned about protecting themselves. In such cases, they will become metaphorical roadblocks, just as Matt is a literal roadblock.

A "Matt" will often want someone to take up his cause for him: to hear his story and declare that his pain is due to an injustice done to him. Unfortunately, this often has the effect of elevating his story of martyrdom. The more effective strategy is to listen, to acknowledge the reality of the pain, and to seek ways to heal or redeem it going forward, as the past is beyond changing.

(continued on the next page...)

(ORGANIZATIONS... continued...)

Ultimately, this has to happen before Matt can be safe to work alongside others, much less lead; as spiritual teacher Richard Rohr has said, "If we do not transform our pain, we will most certainly transmit it." On the other hand, those leaders who acknowledge and seek healing for their own pain can often become the most effective and most trusted. They know what it feels like.

For more discussion on the pain of leadership, see *Leading with a Limp: Take Full Advantage of Your Most Powerful Weakness*, by Dan B. Allender.

Lee the Leader shouted up to Scott the Squatter, "Well, get down then and check it out!"

Scott grumbled to himself about this major inconvenience, but then hopped off the front side of the Rock to take a closer look.

"Are you hurt?" Scott asked the man lying prone on the road, with the massive Rock wedged up against the left side of his body.

"I certainly am! I am hurt from a lifetime of disappointment." He unwedged himself with difficulty and rose unsteadily to his feet. "I'm here because of the Rock. They call me Matt the Martyr and my mission in life is to stop Rocks from rolling. I'm a victim. I'm desperate for you to see and feel my pain. I live and breathe the mantra that 'Rock Rollers Exploit People.' Especially people like me. I want everyone to join my just and worthy cause, which, as you just heard, is me."

But all Lee heard was, "I'm here because of the Rock."

Gloria the Glory Hound thought it would be good public relations to help Matt the Martyr, so she put his arms around her shoulders and helped him to the side of the road. She gave him a drink of water, pulled out some bandages, and tried to calm him down with her best soothing voice. Of course, she was also documenting the entire story on her blog, complete with pictures, mostly selfies.

Lee was frustrated with the waste of time and was about to say something when Bob gave some quick directions. The others all jumped back to work and in no time had the Rock rolling forward again.

Why is Bob giving the orders around here? groused Lee to himself. *I'm the Leader!* But he kept those thoughts to himself because the Rock was, indeed, rolling and that was what he had wanted. It rolled for only a few minutes, however, when suddenly it again came screeching to a halt, as much as slow-rolling Rocks can screech.

"You have got to be kidding me!" shouted Lee from the back of the Rock. He wasn't much good at hiding his frustration in certain cases. And this was as certain a case as ever.

"You have hit a bump in the road," came an unfamiliar woman's voice from the other side of the Rock.

"What?! Another one?" screamed Lee.

"Yep. The path is real bumpy here. Don't you know that?"

WILLIAM'S WISDOM

SAYING NO TO NEGATIVITY

"Negative Nancy" is like "Matt the Martyr" in some respects. She, too, has either been hurt by organizational life or has found it inadequate to her expectations. But Nancy's cynicism may run deeper than her experience with organizations; many of those who are negative at work are also negative in other areas of life. They bring their bitterness, pessimism, or unpleasantness to the job, and thus make the work environment difficult for others, especially their leaders.

The best way to deal with Negative Nancy is not to hire her in the first place! Intentional behavioral interviews and careful use of references can sometimes weed out negative people in the hiring process.

(continued on the next page...)

(SAYING NO TO NEGATIVITY continued...)

But if they're already present (or, worse, if you have a dysfunctional organization that breeds negativity!), there are only three strategies available: termination, isolation, or attitude adjustment. The third is the ideal solution, of course, and a wise, gentle leader can sometimes invite a change in perspective and attitude on the part of someone who has seldom experienced that. Ultimately, however, this choice belongs to Nancy herself, and no one else can make it for her. Otherwise, it may be possible to isolate Nancy so that her negativity has minimum impact on others, but this is warranted only if her output is such to justify her continuance.

(continued on the next page...)

(SAYING NO TO NEGATIVITY continued...)

Creating an organizational culture that minimizes negativity is good for everyone. A healthy organizational culture becomes organically self-correcting; that is, people within the organization instinctively address negative attitudes or behaviors, often without leadership intervention, because they want to protect a positive workplace environment for themselves and others. Leadership is critical for creating this kind of culture but, ultimately, it requires buy-in from the majority of participants. When successful, the difference is palpable. These become the places at which employees truly want to work. They find themselves fulfilled in such places, not stymied.

For more discussion on dealing with negativity in the workplace, see *The No Complaining Rule: Positive Ways to Deal with Negativity at Work,* by Jon Gordon.

And she was right. There was a bump in their path, and the Rock had settled into a depression right in front of it. It was going to take some real work to get it moving in either direction.

"Looks like you're not going anywhere! And, you know, maybe that's best."

"What? How could that be best? This Rock needs to be moving!"

Gloria snapped a quick photo of the woman. "Who are you? I need a name for the Facebook post."

"I'm Nancy. Negative Nancy is what they call me. I plant the seed of doubt wherever I can. Gossip, backstabbing, and a putting a negative spin on everything is what I do best. I will fight tooth and nail to keep this Rock from crossing the Finish Line. But most of the time I won't be overt in my opposition. I'll mostly sabotage you from behind the scenes. My motive, you ask?"

They didn't.

"Well, if you all succeed, I'm afraid that that will highlight all my previous failures, and that's a long list. I just hate to feel bad about myself. It's very simple, really."

Her lips kept moving, but Lee wasn't listening. He was trying to figure out how to get the Rock out of its hole and over the bump. He did notice the persistent scowl on Nancy's face however.

Negative Nancy kept going. "So I suggest that you all call it a day. I mean, you really don't have what it takes to succeed. Especially you, Mr. Leader. That may sound harsh but, really, I'm only looking out for you," she finished with a sardonic half-grin that was more frightening than assuring.

Missy leaned over to Scott. "She really is negative, isn't she?"

But before Scott could answer, Gloria let out a scream! "Ahhhh!!"

The group jumped in unison, then turned, startled to find another man standing among them. Just out of the blue another person had seemingly materialized in front of them!

"Where did you come from?" Gloria exclaimed as she caught her breath.

"Oooh you scared me!" cried Missy at the same time.

"Who in the world are you?" Bob demanded.

"Haha! It's like you didn't even know I was here, wasn't it? Ooh, I love that! I'm Wally the Watcher. I like to remain in the shadows and play it safe. When I am finally seen, my favorite role is to criticize under the guise of 'creative direction.' To be honest, I'm pretty much driven by my fear of failure. To me, safety is key and that generally means watching from a distance and finding problems, even when there aren't any."

Bob groaned under his breath.

But Lee said, "Nice to be watched by you, Wally!" He had heard nothing that Wally said, captivated as he was by the prospect of another team member who could perhaps help the Rock move faster. "Will you be joining us?"

"Well, I wouldn't call it 'joining' really," muttered Wally, "but I'll be right here with you."

Bob spoke up again. "Okay, team, let's get at it! There's work to be done!" Glancing over at Lee, he smiled, "What a large crew we now have! Maybe we can push this Rock over that bump!" But Lee was so upset that Behind the Scenes Bob was giving orders again that he could only nod in agreement.

WILLIAM'S WISDOM

WORKPLACE VOYEUR

Some organizations are like the old carnival game "whack-a-mole." If you stick your head up with a creative idea, you're likely to be punched back down. That doesn't feel good. After a few attempts at this, you learn to duck your head and keep quiet.

Even when an organization invites creativity and risk-taking, some will still be afraid, having learned from past experience in the workplace, or in life in general, not to participate. Instead, they will assume a passive role, becoming a watcher of the efforts of other people. If those others are successful, the watchers will often become jealous of achievements they themselves were too cautious to attempt.

Sometimes watchers obsess what others are doing, becoming workplace voyeurs, intent on knowing (and if possible, stopping) the creative ideas of others so the watcher does not have to deal with the prospect of additional personal failure.

(continued on the next page...)

(WORKPLACE VOYEUR continued...)

Their hope is that all would play things safe, so that no one would stand out as successful and no one would be noticed as a failure. This, of course, is a poor strategy for organizations and people alike.

Sometimes the best way to deal with watchers is to notice that the organization itself is at fault; it unduly penalizes those who stick their heads up. When the organization is deemed safe for new ideas and perspectives, some watchers will engage, cautiously but gratefully. (It is possible that this experience may be truly wonderful for someone who has never felt safe in an organization before and may heal old wounds.)

Many times, however, watchers will never feel safe enough and will insist on creating a very secure environment for their work; if they are able to be appropriately productive with mundane tasks, there may be a place for them in an otherwise fertile work environment. In other cases, however, watchers need to move on, for their fear of failure will disempower both themselves and others from the best that could be achieved.

There are many fine books on overcoming a fear of failure. On leading in a culture of negativity, see *Love Leadership: The New Way to Lead in a Fear-Based World*, by John Hope Bryant.

So all of them got into place and Bob yelled "Push!" But the Rock never even budged.

Something was obviously wrong. Lee looked around at all of them - a full team now - and noticed what the something was - a whole lot of nothing.

He saw Scott the Squatter sitting motionless on top of the Rock. Missy Misguider was pushing the Rock with all her might, but not in the right direction. Gloria the Glory Hound had one hand on the right side of the Rock and the other stretched out, taking a selfie. Wally the Watcher was doing what he did best: watching from a distance. Matt the Martyr was lying in front of the Rock again, sobbing. Behind the Scenes Bob wasn't behind the scenes anymore; he was running from one team member to another, yelling directions. But no one was really paying attention to him anymore. In other words, it was a mess.

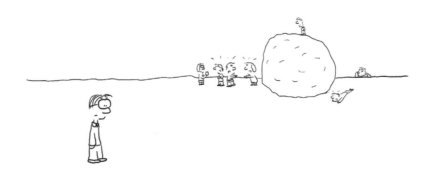

This Rock certainly wasn't going anywhere. It was at a standstill for sure. He couldn't understand what had happened.

Just then Negative Nancy slinked up to Lee the Leader and whispered in his ear, "I bet you volunteered for this, didn't you? You were set up to fail, don't you think? You're a failure. Why don't you just quit this and go home?"

Lee, who usually wasn't listening, heard her loud and clear.

He looked at the confused situation in front of him, then at Nancy, then at the Rock, and just sighed. It may have been the deepest, saddest sigh of his life. Maybe she was right. Maybe he was done.

Lee decided to take a step back and look at the whole picture. Something that he had not done before.

WILLIAM'S WISDOM

HEARING THE WORST?

As we have noted, Lee the Leader is not a good listener, which, incidentally, is not that uncommon among organizational leaders. But this time he actually listens. Why? Because he is in a moment of crisis and does not know what to do. This looks, on the surface, to be one of the worst experiences a leader can have. Truthfully, however, it can often turn out to be a tremendous opportunity.

Crises happen when our customary ways of thinking and acting do not work anymore, when they're not up to the challenge of the moment. We all have our pet ways of dealing with things, and those who are appointed to leadership positions have often mastered those ways; they have become effective at using them. But our usual methods are not the only methods, and from time to time we encounter situations in which something else is called for. When we discover this, we can fall quickly into despair, fearing that we are not up to the task. Any voice that seems to confirm this is amplified in our own mind.

(continued on the next page...)

(HEARING THE WORST continued...)

But a crisis can be a leader's finest moment if we are courageous enough to see things from a new perspective or to try a new way of doing things. This requires courage because we often have to admit that the "tried and true" is no longer working; the organization might even have to reverse course because we have led it down a blind alley. The courage to admit failure and mistakes is still rare among positional leaders but is nearly universal among the leaders most trusted and revered. It bespeaks an authenticity, an unwillingness to pose or pretend and a willingness to learn. And people will trust and follow authenticity.

For more discussion about authenticity, courage, and responsibility in leadership, see Edwin H. Friedman, *A Failure of Nerve: Leadership in the Age of the Quick Fix* (revised edition).

Even Lee could tell this wasn't the way it should be. He decided to do what Any Good Leader would do: Call a meeting and assert his leadership. It was time to address all these issues. It was time to teach these so-called 'team players' a thing or two. "Come here, you all. I've got something to say."

Lee started in and he wasn't bashful. "Look, I am the Leader here, and from what I can see, you guys stink. You have some major issues, team. And I'm using that last word lightly, because I don't see you acting like a team. Not at all. So here's what you're going to do…"

"Gloria, put your phone down and be an actual helper for a change!"

"Scott, get your butt down here with the rest of us and help us roll the Rock. You're just dead weight up there!"

"Missy, why are you pushing in the wrong direction? Yes, you've got lots of energy but it's no good to us if you're working against us. Why can't you see that?"

"Nancy, just shut up! We don't need your cynicism right now."

"And, Matt, for the love of all that is rolling, why are you back on the ground?!"

Lee stopped to catch his breath but Gloria jumped in. "Uh, don't forget Wally. Don't you want to attack him too?"

Wally interrupted. "It's okay. I'll just hang back here and watch. This is fun."

Lee cast him a withering look but said nothing.

He turned next to Behind the Scenes Bob, who was staring with mouth agape. He had worked with Lee for years but had never seen a temper tantrum quite like this. "And you! There's something called a chain of command around here. I don't think you understand it, and I don't think you know how to respect it." Eyes wide in obvious bewilderment, Bob started stuttering something. Lee cut him off. "I need you to go scout out the terrain. Survey everything for the next half mile in front of us, to the side of us, and behind us."

WILLIAM'S WISD⬤M

TEMPER TANTRUMS

When did you last throw a temper tantrum? And did it solve anything in the long run? An expression of pure frustration or bottled anger may be cathartic; it may even create temporary momentum, as frightened employees scamper to do what they're told. But study after study has revealed that temper tantrums are seldom effective over the long term in motivating people, much less building trust or respect.

Truth be told, while there are always exceptions to every rule, most who resort to temper tantrums are not, in the moment, attempting effective leadership; they are blowing steam for their own sake, just like Lee in the story. And, in the end, they do more damage than was already done.

(Continued on the next page...)

(TEMPER TANTRUMS continued...)

Anger, expressed outwardly or not, is rarely helpful at work or in any other aspect of our lives. It erodes our emotional well-being, it destroys relationships, it breeds violence, and it makes us miserable. Beyond even the implications for leadership, it's best to find healthy ways to process the inevitable frustrations, pains, and grievances that tempt us toward anger. Professional help is often valuable in understanding our anger and developing new patterns.

There are many fine books on personal anger management. Ike Lasater and Julie Stiles offer a helpful guide to applying the principles of nonviolent communication to the workplace in *Words That Work In Business: A Practical Guide to Effective Communication in the Workplace*.

"But that doesn't make any sen--" Bob tried to say before being cut off again.

"Go!" barked Lee, and then turned his back away. Bob, stunned at being told off by his friend, in front of the team no less, stormed off to do his meaningless task, muttering ominously as he went.

An awkward silence lingered in the field. Spent of his anger, now Lee could sense the awkwardness too, but he was hardly about to admit it. There was no turning back now. "Let's get back to rolling that Rock. Now!" But even he had little enthusiasm left for the job.

Well, all this drama was the last straw for Gloria, who usually liked drama, but not the kind that made her look bad. Within seconds, she was sending emails and leaving voice-mails, detailing her utter disappointment with all involved, especially Lee the Unleaderly Leader.

"Wow. This doesn't look good," Nancy offered, almost gleefully.

"Why are you even here? And why are you so against this project?" Lee erupted.

"Yeah, not good at all." Nancy smirked.

A dejected Lee took another glance at the Rock. His Rock. He took a deep breath. And then another. He knew he had only made things worse. No one was pushing anything. Some were in shock. Most were sitting on the ground, eyes downward. But he had no clue how to make things better. He had no words to utter. And he had no plan to get the Rock over the hump.

Suddenly, the vision of a long white beard appeared in his mind. "Maybe that William the Wise guy would know what to do with these problem rollers! Maybe he can help me straighten them out." Leaving his team in chaos, Lee hurried off to find that trail again.

When Lee arrived, sweating and out of breath, William the Wise was still on his porch, seemingly waiting for him. "You're back? So I expected. But so soon! Things are not so good, eh?"

"No, not good at all. We're stuck. And no one is listening to me. They don't know how to follow…that's the problem!"

WILLIAM'S WISD⊙M

A PROBLEM OF FOLLOWERSHIP OR LEADERSHIP?

No one leads without being followed by at least someone. If no one is following, is that because of a problem of followership or a problem of leadership?

As with most such dualisms, the answer is "either or both." Sometimes excellent leadership is present and few see it or want it. The adage that "we get the leaders we deserve" has some merit. And yet we must also recognize that our world is crying out for leadership. Most don't know entirely what, exactly, they are looking for, but there remains a desperate hope for someone (or a group of someones) to take leadership and effectively address the many challenges of our world.

(continued on the next page...)

**(A PROBLEM OF FOLLOWERSHIP
OR LEADERSHIP continued...)**

As journalist Thomas Friedman has pointed out, the world has gotten "flat," in terms of access to information and to each other. This flatness has resulted, not in the homogenization that earlier cultural theorists had predicated, but even greater tribalism, as partisans and fans of any cause can now more easily find each other.

Seth Godin has noted that when they do come together they look for leaders. It is not difficult in the twenty-first century to be a leader, if all that is required is followers; it is immensely difficult, however, to be a truly effective leader, when one's followers have open, even intimate, access to the behaviors of other leaders. Comparison and contrast are inevitable, and sometimes brutal.

In such circumstances, it does one little good to blame the follower for not being astute enough to recognize the wisdom of the leader; it is more important that the leader demonstrate the good sense to seek the wisdom of the followers.

For more discussion, see *The World is Flat: A Brief History of the Twenty-First Century, by Thomas L. Friedman, and Tribes: We Need You to Lead Us,* by Seth Godin.

Wise William just kept rocking slowly and continued to listen, his face betraying nothing. "Please come and sit down with me, Leland," he said, pointing toward a chair.

Lee sat down but continued talking frantically. "No one is doing what they should be doing. Oh, sure, Bob gets them moving pretty well. But Bob's not the Leader. I am! Why aren't they following me??"

William, like usual, took his time in responding. "Is it possible that you are more interested in building your reputation and resume than building a team that functions well? Is it possible that you are more concerned about being called the Leader instead of being the leader? After all, what does a title mean in this journey of leadership? It often means very little. There are many leaders who never have titles, and many with titles who are never truly leaders."

"What matters is directing your team effectively, so that they not only get the job done but become better people in the process. Notice who they are, and not just what they do. And then focus on what they do best, not what they do worst. Use their best gifts and talents, and they will do more than you ever thought possible."

WILLIAM'S WISD🐑M

LEARNING FROM FOLLOWERS?

Learning is a multi-directional process. Yes, leaders have a responsibility to help their followers grow, and team members can and should help each other. But few leaders appear to be confident enough to permit their followers to teach them a thing or two. This requires considerable vulnerability but can make the difference between continuing to act out of one's self-deception or blind spot and becoming a truly effective and trustworthy leader.

Followers have much to teach leaders in part because many of them are leaders themselves, even if they do not bear a title. Leadership is diffused throughout each organization, albeit often unnoticed by those at the center or the top. In fact, the most transformative leadership is often found at the margins. If you think about, those who make it to the top of a pyramid usually do so by mastering the status quo, not by changing paradigms. (There are always exceptions, of course!)

(continued on the next page...)

(LEARNING FROM FOLLOWERS continued...)

Those in the organization who are critiquing the dominant paradigm may indeed be among the most creative leaders you have, even if among the most unpopular as well. So let them lead in their own way; they will not seek typically seek to undermine your own leadership but will want to be heard. And often they have something to teach those who stand in the center of things.

For more discussion on leading from the margins, see *Boundary Leaders* by Gary R. Gunderson. For discussion on effective followership, see *Followership: How Followers Are Creating Change and Changing Leaders*, by Barbara Kellerman.

No one had ever talked to Lee like this before. But he was listening intently, capturing each word, testing each idea in his mind. He was desperate, and he knew it. And this time, he was humble. Far more humble than his last visit. William could see the turmoil on Lee's face.

"As I told you before, the Great Truth of Rock Rolling, the Great Truth of all worthwhile endeavors, is this: Let each member of your team show you how they work best. They will seldom come out and say it. Most of them don't even know it consciously themselves. But if you listen to them and watch them, if you get to know them as people and not just as Rock pushers, you will come to understand their motivations, their stories, and their strengths.

You will see all their goodness and not just all their weaknesses. And, by the way, if you let them, they will help you understand your own strengths and weaknesses as well. And then, you will know how, where, and when each can best serve. You will know how they can best work together to roll the Rock. But you must listen, Lee. If you want to be the Leader, you must first listen."

And, then, with a touch of gentleness, William finished: "I tried to tell you this the last time. But, ironically, you weren't listening."

Lee thought about all that William had said. He really thought. He thought until his head hurt. William waited patiently. Slowly a smile warmed across Lee's face. Then a simple "Thank you" came from his lips. And he meant it. Then he shook William's hand and, with the same hurry with which he had come, he abruptly left.

William called after him, "Leland, remember: Your people have already told you how to roll the Rock. You just need to listen to them. Listen to what motivates them." And then he leaned back in his rocker, a gleam in his eye.

On his way down the trail, Lee felt different. He was determined to try what William the Wise had said. In fact, as Lee scurried back down the trail, he started to think about how he had acted as a young, aspiring leader. And how he had been treated by other leaders. Some of it hadn't been good. He had scars from those years of rock rolling. Wounds that he had to overcome and let heal. And it startled him to think that he was now the one wounding others.

Lee even started to think about what motivated him. He had to admit to himself that his own motives were mixed. He liked public praise more than he should. He enjoyed building his resume. He wanted greater respect and more responsibility in the future. But he discovered that he also truly wanted to be a good Leader. He truly wanted to be the kind of person that others would trust, that people would want to follow. As he thought of it, what had given him greatest satisfaction in the leadership role he had already filled was helping people grow, developing others. Several faces crossed his mind...rock-rollers who were once members of teams he had led but now lead teams of their own. He smiled at the thought of it.

Before he was even halfway back, he had made up his mind that he was going to do what Wise William had said. As each of his rock rollers came to mind he considered how he would talk to them. "No, no," he reminded himself, how he would listen to them. And how he would remember what they had already told him, through words and actions, about themselves.

Foremost on his mind was Bob, now truly behind the scenes, sent off into near-exile through Lee's temper and jealousy. Lee wanted to clear the air with him, to apologize to his old friend, who had recently become a new enemy.

When Lee finally returned to his team, he found the Rock exactly as he had left it: massive and unmoved. And he found his team, minus Bob, as he had left them: silent and sulking. Each was leaning against the Rock, facing outward, not daring to look in each other's eyes, unwilling or unable to act.

No one saw him coming so Lee stopped in his tracks and observed his team members with a new fondness, and smiled. He took a deep breath, then approached cautiously, not wanting to frighten them. He spoke with Gloria the Glory Hound first. He looked deeply into her eyes and said softly, "Gloria, you do know that you are able to offer something unique and wonderful to this team, right?" Gloria swelled with pride, although she tried to hide it at first. "You are the glue that holds us together. You make hard work fun. And you are a great supporter of our work."

WILLIAM'S WISD◉M

MORE THAN JUST GETTING THE JOB DONE

One of the important reminders that the dominant leadership models of our generation offer us is that leadership is not merely about the accomplishment of certain goals, tasks, and objectives. It is also about influencing other people for their own good. It is about building capacity in followers. It is about providing meaning to accompany one's labor. It is about making the world a better place. This is why we say that leadership ultimately has a redemptive goal.

Some may scoff at such language as overly idealistic, but the researchers and advocates of transformational and servant leadership, in particular, suggest that such goals are not only appropriate but even necessary for effective long-term leadership. Leadership that exploits or uses, that treats humans merely as "resources" to do a job, is not only harmful to one's self and others but also ultimately ineffective. (Can we eliminate the phrase "human resources" from our workplaces, please?)

(continued on the next page...)

(MORE THAN JUST GETTING
THE JOB DONE continued...)

The primary output to be observed or even measured, they argue, is the effect one's leadership has on the lives of one's followers. No one has argued this more passionately than Robert Greenleaf, the father of the "servant leadership" movement that has inspired thousands in the past generation. His argument was simply that if one wishes to be a good leader, one must first be a good servant of those one leads. It sounds paradoxical, but such servant leadership makes people want to follow. It's what generates trust, and without trust there is no true leadership, only the exercise of power.

For more discussion, see *Servant Leadership: A Journey into the Nature of Legitimate Power and Greatness*, by Robert K. Greenleaf.

"That's all I want to do!" Gloria cried. "I want to make the other team members feel good about what they do. When people feel good about their jobs, they do better. They enjoy life more."

"You are right!" exclaimed Lee the Leader. Gloria swelled with pride again, and this time she didn't try to hide it. Lee then said, "I know you are good at public relations when things are going well, but do you think you can be a cheerleader for us at all times? Can you encourage us even when things are not going well? Maybe even especially then?"

"Yeah, sure. I can do that."

Lee added, "Wonderful! And, by the way, we're here for you too. If you don't bail on us, we won't bail on you."

"You got it!" Gloria smiled. "I'll tell everyone what we talked about." She got quickly to her feet with a fresh energy and hurried away to get to work.

Lee then moved around the Rock to find Missy Misguider, still slightly sweaty as she sat with her back to the Rock. He was amazed to find that she was still trying to push it, all by herself, even in her dejected mood. "Hi Missy! Wow… watching you, I believe that you were born to roll Rocks! You really have a passion for this, don't you?"

Missy blushed, then said, "Well, I guess so, Lee. I mean I totally love this project. I love rolling Rocks. I love working as a team. I'd probably do this work for nothing, but it seems that I always mess things up. I'm no good at the very thing I love doing." She looked so sad Lee thought her heart would break.

"So what do you need, Missy? How can I help you?"

Missy hardly missed a beat. "I have no sense of direction. All I really need, I think, is to be told where to roll and in what direction. And then I'm good to go."

"Excellent! We can do that! I'll ask the others to help you push in the right direction. But I'm also giving you permission to come to me at any time. If you need help, if you're not sure of something, just ask me instead of waiting for it. I will not criticize you for that; in fact, I'll be glad that you asked. You are empowered from this moment forward."

"Thank you! That's really all I need." By this time Missy was nearly squealing with delight.

Lee squeezed her hand and started to rise. "Oh, and the next point we're rolling to is that way," he pointed.

"Oh, okay." Missy replied, a sheepish grin on her face.

Lee stood up and walked over to Scott, who was squatting beside the Rock staring upward at the sky. "Now Scott, I understand you have your own agenda and it's not about rolling this Rock. But if you insist on squatting on top of the Rock all the time, none of us, yourself included, are getting where we want to be."

"I can see your point. Go on," said Scott cautiously.

"Well, for instance, where do you want to go? Maybe we can go together? Can we create a win-win here?"

Scott mused for a moment. "Well, maybe. While I can't ignore my own agenda, I don't see why I can't also support yours. You are going my way, so I'll go along with you. That's all I can give you."

Lee nodded his head in agreement. "Okay, I'm good with that. But you can't ride. You need to push, along with everyone else. You can't just sit up top doing squat."

"I suppose. We'll probably get there more quickly if I helped out too."

"Exactly my point." Lee smiled, then almost immediately bent down to speak with Matt the Martyr, who was not exactly lying down, but was huddled on the ground in his favorite spot, in front of the Rock.

"Matt," Lee started in, "I understand you have been hurt in the past. I can't change what's already been done, but I can assure you about what we're doing here and now. I would never think of hurting you or exploiting you. I don't work like that. I can't promise that everybody will always treat you right all the time, but I can promise that we'll do our best to make sure you are well taken care of. What would that look like to you? What do you need from me to feel safe and be productive?"

Matt looked back at Lee in astonishment. "I never had a Leader ask me that before. Thank you. To be honest, I want to be on the back side of the Rock, so I will never get run over again. It's really scary on any other side. I go out front because that's the only way I can get the Rock to stop moving."

Lee nodded in agreement. "That sounds great. It's where we need you most anyway. You can go to the back right now, if you wish. You'll be safe there."

Matt jumped up excitedly. "You know, I've got a good sense of direction. Maybe I can help steer back there too?"

Lee laughed. "Actually, Missy needs some help steering. Can you work alongside her? She'll look out for you and you can look out for her."

"Sounds great, boss!"

Lee stood up and looked around, confusion on his face. "Where's Wally? I'd like to talk to him next." Everyone looked around. "Wally who?" Apparently Wally the Watcher had left without anyone noticing. "Well," said Lee, "That's what Watchers do. We're all better off."

"Do you really think all this happy talk is going to help? I mean, really—" The voice of Negative Nancy was a shrill as ever.

"Nancy, I already know the answer to this question, but I'll ask it anyway. Are you able to fully support this project?" Lee asked. "I'm glad to help you flourish here, but you'll need to commit along with the others, and to participate without negative talk or actions. Will you?"

Nancy glared at Lee for ten long seconds. Then, slowly, she turned and walked away without a word. She even kicked some dirt in front of the Rock on her way past. In an instant, she was gone, much to everyone's delight.

Lee looked at his team. He sighed. "We're missing Bob. Is he still out there somewhere doing that meaningless task I gave him?"

"I think, actually, he is checking on his other rocks," Gloria offered. "You upset him quite a bit, you know."

"I know. Go ahead and start rolling, everyone. That direction," he said. "I'll be back." Lee the Leader then went out in search of his old friend. Through fields and fields, he looked. He was exhausted, but he wasn't going to give up.

Finally, in a distant field, Lee the Leader spotted Bob, busy at work on another rock. He walked up to him quietly and carefully. When Bob finally saw him, Lee blurted, "Bob, before you say anything, I want you to know that I realized that I've been a bad Leader and a bad friend. And I want to apologize."

"Go on."

WILLIAM'S WISD☁M

STUBBORNNESS OR PERSISTENCE

An oft-quoted inspirational anecdote told at leadership seminars is that of Winston Churchill urging the young men of Britain to persevere in the face of danger: "Never give in, never give in, never, never, never, never—in nothing, great or small, large or petty!" Seldom, however, is the rest of Churchill's sentence quoted: "Never give in except to convictions of honor and good sense."

The caveat he offered may be commonly overlooked but is essential to good leadership. There is, after all, a difference between stubborn, unyielding intransigence in the face of information that contradicts what one wishes to be true, and the kind of persistence that holds fast to the objective until or unless there is a moral or rational reason...something right or wise...for changing course. And there are many good moral and rational reasons for changing course!

(continued on the next page...)

(STUBBORNNESS OR PERSISTENCE continued...)

In fact, the ability to be flexible, even agile, in the means one uses to achieve objectives is a key characteristic of a 21st-century leader. Largely gone are the days of the detailed five-year plans; there are simply too many factors beyond the power of the leader or the organization to influence. Our illusion of control has been shattered, but it was only an illusion anyway.

The kind of leadership needed now is that of someone who can think on his or her feet, who can quickly imagine and implement alternatives when roadblocks appear, who can emotionally detach oneself from a particular method or even outcome in order to achieve what is possible (or even better) in the circumstances as they are. This, too, requires a certain perseverance, but it's a creative perseverance, not a refusal to be moved. It's an exercise of the imagination, not just of the will. And imagination will be a key characteristic of effective leadership in this century.

For more discussion on agility in leadership and organizations, see *The Fifth Discipline: The Art and Practice of the Learning Organization*, by Peter M. Senge.

"I'm sorry for being jealous of your abilities. I'm sorry for losing my temper. I'm sorry for that stupid assignment I gave you. I'm sorry for not listening well."

Bob was taken aback. He had expected one of those "sorry if I did something that upset you" pseudo-apologies. But Lee was being serious and specific. This sounded very sincere. Bob relaxed, remembering the genial, trustworthy Leader he had usually known Lee to be. He stretched out his hand to firmly pump Lee's, the handshake giving affirmation to the single word he uttered: "Forgiven."

Lee breathed deeply and gladly. "May I ask you a question?"

"Sure."

"You are so good at helping others do their jobs, Bob. But what do you need? How can I be a better Leader to you?"

Bob was stunned. Lee had never asked him that kind of question before. In fact, no Leader had ever asked him anything remotely like that before. They were all concerned about how Bob could help them, not the other way around. But Lee's earnest expression showed that he really wanted an answer.

Bob decided to risk it. "I need you to trust me, Lee. I need authority to fulfill the responsibility you have given me as your second in command. If you let me do what I do best, we'll both be better off."

Lee cast his gaze downward in embarrassment. "Well, sometimes, to be honest, I feel threatened by you." He hadn't intended to say that. He was ashamed to admit it. But there it was…

"What?" Bob replied. "You have nothing to fear from me. I don't want to be the Leader of this project. I don't even like being a leader on my smaller projects. That's not something I have aspired to. I don't like having overall responsibility. I really prefer to work behind the scenes. I'm pretty good at implementing the plans that others create, which is why you and I usually work together really well."

Lee smiled at him gratefully. "Bob, you're right. I'm sorry I didn't trust you. Please come back with me. I've made some necessary changes, but even with those, this Rock won't get anywhere without you by my side."

Bob asked, "Do you think the team is going to be mad at me for leaving them?"

"No, I don't think so," Lee laughed. "If they're not mad at me for yelling at them, they certainly won't be mad at you."

"They're not mad at you anymore?"

"Come on, I have something to show you."

Lee led Bob back to the Rock. But it wasn't where Lee had left it. They followed its tracks down the path for a while until they finally caught up with it. The Rock was still rolling and everyone was pushing.

Behind the Scenes Bob stopped in his tracks. "Wow! They've rolled the Rock so far in so little time! What did you do? How did you know what to do? What to say to them?"

Lee laughed. "It wasn't what *I* said that mattered. It was what *they* said." Then Lee told him of the story of William the Wise and his mountain home. And the Rock that sat beside it. **Most importantly, he told Bob the Great Truth that William the Wise had shared with him: "Listen to your people and they will tell you how they serve best. Listen to what motivates them."**

And as Lee told Bob about the Great Truth, Bob was surprised to see a gleam in Lee's eyes that had never been there before. Bob was suddenly very excited about this. "I want to do my best for you! And if you listening to your people works such miracles, I can do the same."

Bob grew more serious.

"Thanks, Lee. As I think about it, I realize I need to back down sometimes. If I see something that can be done better, I sure want to fix it. And in a hurry. I said you should have trusted me. But I should have trusted you to be the leader, instead of just taking over. I'm sorry."

Lee put a hand on Bob's shoulder. "All is forgiven. Thank you."

"Any way I can help you, let me know. I want to be a support to you, Lee. I'll even let you be the leader!" Bob and Lee shared a laugh, old friends once again.

Lee the Leader knew then and there that there was hope. Hope for him to become a truly great Leader. Hope for his team to not only succeed at their task but to find some healing and goodness in accomplishing it. What William the Wise had said had turned out to be true, and the happy results were right before Lee's eyes. It wouldn't be long before he and his team rolled that Rock all the way to its final destination. Permanently.

Off in the distance, William the Wise rocked on his porch and smiled knowingly. If someone had been there, they would have seen a strange and happy gleam in his eye.

WILLIAM'S WISDOM

THE GLEAM IN YOUR EYE?

Do others see a gleam in your own eye? Some hard-won wisdom or deep insight that you now have to offer others, drawn from your own experience?

There is nothing special about William the Wise; he was not gifted with supernatural rock-rolling abilities, easy terrain, or perfect rocks. He faced the same challenges as other leaders. But he emerged both more successful and wiser than most, simply because he was willing to face failure and learn from it. And now he has something to give to those who take up the same task. They, too, of course, will need to learn from their own failures, just as Lee the Leader has done in this little fable.

Lee is developing his own gleam in the process. How about you?

ABOUT THE AUTHORS

A native of rural Lancaster county, Pennsylvania and graduate of small town, USA, **Dr. Clayton Stitzel** has served in and assisted with numerous non-profit organizations with local, national, and international focuses. Dedicating his professional career to the advancement in the field of treating idiopathic scoliosis has created a unique array of leadership opportunities which he has incorporated into this literary effort. Blessed with a loving wife and children, Dr. Stitzel continues to learn, develop, and promote best practices in leadership and team building.

Dr. Tony Blair has been leading faith-based nonprofit organizations for nearly 35 years, leading teams of mission-driven staff and volunteers to "roll rocks" of all sizes and shapes. He is currently President and Dean of Evangelical Seminary in Myerstown, Pennsylvania, and Senior Pastor of Hosanna! A Fellowship of Christians in Lititz, Pennsylvania. He has authored numerous articles and books on leadership and related matters, trying to preach what he practices. He and his wife Carol live in Lancaster County, Pennsylvania.

Paul De Rose has been involved in the creative arts for over 25 years. As an actor, writer, director and producer, he has created and developed a wide variety of projects. He has worked for Universal Studios, Paramount Pictures and Sight & Sound Theatres in Lancaster, Pennsylvania. He has led many teams, most often in the areas of production, but his happiest moments come when he is using comedy to tell intriguing, redemptive stories. Paul lives in Lancaster County with his wife, their two children, and a dog who also loves comedy.